'Parenting Techniques'

Successful Parenting of Children and Teenagers With Challenging Behaviour, ADHD & Asperger's

By Dan Jones

Contact the Author

www.discoverdanjones.co.uk , www.personalfreedom.co.uk

Third Edition 2011

First Paperback Edition 2011

Published and Printed By Lulu.com

Copyright © Daniel Jones 2006

Daniel Jones asserts the moral right to be identified as the author of this work

All rights reserved. No part of this publication may be reproduced, stored in a retrieval system, or transmitted, in any form or by any means, electronic, mechanical, photocopying, recording, or otherwise, without the prior written permission of the publishers or author.

ISBN: 978-1-4467-9495-1

3 Third Edition 3

Contents

Introduction	7
Relaxation	15
Boundaries and Consequences	19
Quality of the relationship between you and your child	25
Listening and Communication	29
Help with getting your child to sleep	31
Reducing the risk of aggression	35
An Understanding of Anger and how it controls the mind of the aggressor	39
Basic emotional needs	45
What is necessary to remember when confronted with challenging behaviour	51
Strategies for managing challenging behaviour	55
Finally	65

Introduction

For over 10 years now I have worked extensively with children and young people with emotional and behavioural problems and with parents that are struggling with their children. I have worked with children and the parents of children with a diagnosis of conditions like; Attention Deficit Hyperactivity Disorder (ADHD), Oppositional Defiance Disorder (ODD), Asperger's, Tourette's, and Obsessive Compulsive Disorder (OCD)

For many of those 10 years I worked in residential childcare with children aged 5-18. And in 2004 I also helped to set up a Therapeutic Children's Home and taught the new staff behaviour management skills and techniques.

Frequently what was discovered was that the children formed more positive and open relationships with adults that kept boundaries in place and were consistent than they did with the adults that let them do whatever they wanted.

In my one to one work with families often the person that appears to need to be worked with (normally a child) isn't present and has no desire (expressed) to change, they often like things the way they are. The parent(s) want all the answers on how I can tell them to make their child behave and do exactly as they are told.

I listen to the patterns that occur, pay attention to any basic emotional needs being met inappropriately or not being met at all (for all involved - child, parents, other siblings) and gather as much information as I can.

Often I can feedback something that will have a change on the family situation. For me it is important to get the parents to the point where they are talking about what part they play in the problem. Sometimes people don't want to accept any responsibility and want the child to carry all responsibility on their shoulders. Or they don't realise that they play a part in their current situation.

As the adults are normally the ones motivated to want things to be different it is best for them to see what they can do to change the situation. Many parents say things like 'He makes me so angry' or 'I just get so irritated by her'. My aim is to help parents to take back control and decide how they want to respond, not respond how their child is making them respond.

When I worked in residential childcare with children with severe challenging behaviour if you tell them to stop swearing it wouldn't work, they would do it more, so often I would tell them to swear at me more and would encourage it and get them to try to think of more examples. I would do this in a playful way. It is important that it isn't perceived as being antagonistic.

The young people would often get frustrated at doing as I want them to do and get irritated with having to swear at me more so they would stop. Obviously this would be done skilfully and respectfully so as not to increase aggression, and was done calmly and with a playful attitude and it wasn't done with all young people in all situations.

It is important to note that everyone is different so what skills and techniques you use for one child or young person may not be the same as you would use for another. And what you use at one time may not be appropriate at a different time – perhaps due to the young person's frame of mind at that time or the situation you are in.

Many parents get stuck in their patterns and find that they just continue to repeat the same pattern even when it doesn't work because they don't know what else to try.

I worked with a single dad that used to ground his daughter if he telephoned her to ask her to come home for dinner and she turned out to be outside of the agreed area they lived in. She used to turn her phone off when she was in the wrong so that she didn't get told off. This made her Dad worry because he couldn't contact her so he would ground her for a very long time. She knew that she would get grounded for a long time so didn't want her phone on and wouldn't want to come home. All of which led to the father worrying more and getting increasingly angry and more likely to over-react with the consequences when he finally saw his daughter.

After she had been grounded and was again able to go out she would just carry on doing the same behaviour as she was before. He then reacted to this behaviour by grounding his daughter again and the cycle would continue. No-one could see a way out or an alternative so they continued to make the same choices.

Another common problem is where a solution the parent uses leads to maintaining the problem. For example a parent believing a child shouldn't have the last word, or shouldn't 'get away' with talking to them the way they do; shouts at the child – the child shouts back - the parent shouts at the child - etc (so the solution to shout at the child to tell them off for shouting and swearing is making them shout and swear).

Or a parent pestering a teenager because they never leave their bedroom and so the parent is worried they may be depressed - the teenager stays in their room because the parent is always pestering - parent pesters more because they worry – the teenager withdraws more because they are being pestered - etc.

Many parents already know solutions to their problems they just don't realise it yet. When working with parents they often want a set of instructions. Unfortunately everybody is different so parents can be educated about the principles behind what makes a strategy or consequence work and can then use these principles to continually create new strategies as their child grows up and can also then adapt to changes that will occur as their child goes through different stages of development and different phases of behavioural responses towards the parents.

One example of parents already knowing how to manage a situation but not realising it is when I ask parents about situations and they tell me they didn't know what to do and that they have 'tried everything'. I'll ask 'So what happened?' And will then have the parent describe the whole incident to me right to the point that it ended.

It is important to remember that if a situation ends something has led to that. And if it is a situation that also involved a parent then something the parent did contributed to the situation ending.

When I have been through this process of asking what happened and how did it end parents often say they reached the end of their tether and just walked away. They often see this as a failure yet when I ask 'So then what happened?' They often respond by saying 'they calmed down'.

This calming down may have taken 5 minutes or it may have taken an hour, yet what led to the situation finally calming down was the parent taking control and walking away.

This book is written based on my training in managing challenging behaviour exhibited by children and young people with behavioural difficulties, anger problems, ADHD and children on the Autistic Spectrum, my training in Solution Focused Therapy and my training in a Human Givens Approach to Therapy and my 10 years of experience with children and families both in a residential setting where I successfully applied the information in this book to real situations, and my one to one and group work with parents and families helping them to successfully put these ideas into practice.

The strategies in this book work with children with Attention Deficit Hyperactivity Disorder (ADHD), Oppositional Defiance Disorder (ODD), Asperger's and Angry Behaviour and can help with children with Obsessive Compulsive Disorder (OCD) and Tourette's.

This book has been written to be a quick read. I sometimes recommend books to parents and because parents are often incredibly busy with very hectic lifestyles they feedback that they didn't have time to read the book and wish the book got to the point quicker. Many parents have also fed back to me that they like books that are short enough to be able to go back to and reread sections if they need to quickly recap or learn something so that they can apply it straight away rather than having a situation occur but not reading about how they perhaps should have or be handling those situations until a week or two later.

Relaxation

One of the most important skills for parents to learn and for children is how to relax. When people are relaxed they think clearer. They have an increased tolerance to stress and are less likely to become aggressive.

Generally Tourette's symptoms can be reduced by helping the child to relax more. The more you can help them learn to relax or teach them ways to relax themselves the calmer they can remain and the more control they can have over their symptoms. Likewise with children that stutter.

Helping a child to relax especially from an early age is one of the most useful skills you can teach. There are a variety of ways you can help someone to relax. One of the best techniques is 7-11 breathing. With 7-11 breathing the person breathes in counting to 7 and out counting to 11. The advantages of this technique are that it is something someone can do privately. Some of the children I have worked with have been taught relaxation techniques like clenching their fists and then relaxing them but then the children have refused to use the techniques because they feel stupid if they get seen doing them even though they will say the techniques calm them down.

7-11 breathing works because each time you breathe out you trigger the relaxation response in your body. Normally we breathe in and out evenly so when we breathe in we trigger the stress response then when we breathe out we trigger the relaxation response and this is kept fairly even making us not get too stressed or relaxed.

When people get stressed they often begin to breathe faster and begin to make the in breaths slightly longer than the out breaths increasing the stress experienced and making the person more prone to getting angry or irritated. With 7-11 breathing the person begins to feel calmer and more relaxed the longer the do the technique for. This is useful for children to learn so that as soon as they feel themselves getting worked up they can begin to stop it from escalating. It is also useful for parents so that parents can remain calmer and make better parenting decisions based on calm rational thinking rather than stressed irrational thinking.

Other relaxation ideas include guided meditation where someone can learn to create a pleasant place in their mind and can practice closing their eyes to go to that pleasant place. If the person begins to feel stressed they can then go to their room or find somewhere they can sit or lie down quietly and take some time to close their eyes and go to that place.

Places people use include somewhere they have been on holiday that they liked, or sitting in the country or in a woodland area, or being on a beach. For children sometimes they create fantasy lands to visit.

Parents can relax their children by learning to remain calm and relaxed themselves and being calm and relaxed when managing situations that normally would have led to stress. Likewise they can speak in a relaxed way when reading stories to their children rather than excitedly speaking all the voices and making the reading too lively which then leaves the child more alert and awake and full of energy.

If you are in a situation where you feel yourself getting angry; sit down. If you sit down this is a calm action so it reduces the chances of your behaviour escalating problems at the same time as calming you down and helping you to manage the situation better.

It is also important to relax between 'stresses'. So if you are stressed from a day at work and then instantly picking up screaming children from school you will already be close to snapping point. If you can bring down your stress levels a little even by pulling up in your car somewhere and taking 2 minutes to relax and create a break between work life and home life this will help you to have an increased tolerance to handling stress.

Boundaries and Consequences

We all have boundaries and consequences that we have to follow in our day to day lives. We have to get up at specific times, do specific things during the day, be on time to places, and stick within the law. Many children think that as adults we can do whatever we want. As adults we need to help children to understand boundaries and consequences and why they are in place.

It would be unusual for a child to stick to all boundaries and you want them to grow up feeling comfortable pushing boundaries where appropriate yet understanding the consequences of their actions.

Make house rules that EVERYONE including parents have to stick to. Make sure that everyone was involved in creating these rules and that the rules are positively worded not 'do not...etc'. You want to all agree the consequences of not sticking to the house rules.

Make sure that all consequences are things that you will definitely stick to. Consistency is the key. If you can't stick to something don't set it. Make consequences appropriate to the boundary broken and make them age specific. So a 16 year old coming in drunk may have to clean up any sick (if they were sick) or it may be that the hangover is enough consequence. It would depend on your situation. It maybe that a teenager continually ignores rules and does as they please so parents stop doing things for them like cooking and cleaning leaving them to be independent as this is what they are behaving like they want.

Many parents I have worked with see walking away as failure. This is actually an excellent strategy. If you can walk away do. Useful ideas are: Distraction, Ignoring, Offering Choices, Making clear consequences and sticking to them.

Keep calm, keep your voice calm, don't shout or raise your voice. Try not to use materialistic punishments like taking things away, or materialistic rewards. Always be consistent. Remember once someone is angry they won't see alternatives so don't talk to them about an incident until they are calm (usually many hours later or the next day) and remember that actions speak louder than words so don't push for a verbal sorry, let them be responsible for their actions and decisions, just stick to making clear what is expected of them (not what 'isn't' expected), what the consequences of doing and not doing that are, then carry out the consequences. This is what you are in control of; they are in control of their actions and decisions.

Plan in advance how you will handle situations you can anticipate happening. This stops you needing to think on the spot or raise your voice because you can then stick to repeating the same sentence over and over regardless of what your child says.

A mistake made by many parents is that the child says they don't care about the consequences and so the parent puts something else in place as well as what is already in place. For example a parent may tell the teenager they are grounded. The teenager responds by shouting and swearing and being insulting. The parent now retaliates by saying the grounding is now longer and this continues.

The consequence was already put in place so the parent should just stick to that not add to it. Normally if the child responds by shouting and swearing and being abusive the consequence has got to them. If it doesn't work as a consequence then the parents can rethink for future situations and if necessary come up with a different consequence for then. You would want to have tried the same consequence a number of times before making the decision that it doesn't work; and remember that the child will express that they didn't care and that it didn't work. You don't want to necessarily take this to mean it didn't work. Remember Brer Rabbit and the briar patch where he begged the wolf to do anything but throw him in the briar patch so eventually the wolf threw him in which is what he wanted.

As well as negative consequences you want to have positive consequences. So if the child makes one decision they get a positive outcome, and the other decision they get a negative outcome.

When you give the child a positive outcome you want them to keep it. So if a child earns the privilege of staying up 30 minutes extra on a Friday night but then plays up all Friday you don't want to take what they have earned away from them.

Very often parents feel that a child with a diagnosis of ADHD or Asperger's is likely to need either medication or a specialist parenting style. Normally all that is needed is the same as other children. The difference is that it often needs to be stuck to more rigidly and made very clear to the child.

For example a child with ADHD has a lot of energy to be channelled. Not all children with ADHD have behavioural problems as some have learnt to channel their energy into activities or sports or interests. Parents need to think about what consequences they will put in place and make sure that consequences are what the child enjoys and would want to do.

If the child has ADHD they will have lots of energy, they will be very demanding and time consuming. Every child is different but the common theme is for parents to find ways that meet the child's need to use their energy and usually short attention span. It is important to make consequences very close to boundaries. So if a child is misbehaving you want the consequence to happen now, not saying they won't be able to do something at the weekend or in a few days time.

The child will need to make the connection between boundaries and consequences. They also are likely to have a low attention span so again you want to make sure that you only work within the child's current attention span. If for example they are told to do their homework for an hour then told off 30 minutes later because they are now messing around the parent put the child in a position they were likely to fail. If on the other hand the parent has the child work on something for 5-10 minutes then do something different, then do another 5-10 minutes they are working with the child's natural thinking process and inability to focus on one thing for a long period of time.

Some parents say this is difficult because it is more time consuming for them yet when they start doing this they find it takes up less time than it used to take trying to make them do their homework before.

With children with Asperger's it is important to make boundaries and consequences clear. Routine is very important as is certainty. So if any boundary is vague it is likely to cause anxiety and increase the chances of problem behaviour. Again you want to treat the child in a way that is suitable for the child rather than in a way that the parent perhaps feels should be the way things are done. For example children with Asperger's are less likely to want to make eye contact and may well be uncomfortable with too much physical contact so you want to have them sat beside you both perhaps focusing on some rules when explaining them so that there is no pressure to make eye contact; and not to say things like 'look at me when I'm talking to you'.

I have known parents that are set in their ways and have expectations like having the child look at them when the parent is speaking. Then they tell the child off even though the child was listening in their own way.

It is important to give lots of praise when a child or teenager does something correct never mind how small. Within a day you want to give a minimum of 10 positives/praises for each negative. It has to be honest and specific praise. It could be praising responding in the morning showing they are awake, praising their willingness to be honest with you when telling you something you don't want to hear, praising them for at least attending registration in school even if they walked out straight away after that.

Praise for every little thing that is positive or good behaviour. This demonstrates a positive consequence for good behaviour.

Quality of the relationship between you and your child

Find ways to praise your child regularly even if it is for a very small thing. Put achievements out on display, take photographs of times when your child is being good and together you are having fun. Put these pictures on display.

Imagine positive relationships you had with adults as a child and what made them positive. Think about what your child needs in the relationship.

Write down positives at the end of each day and things that have happened that you want to continue to have happen.

As a family set a task of everyone doing 1,2,3 or more nice things across the week to each other then at the end of the week sit together and tell each other what nice things you noticed. Not what nice things you DID but what you noticed others do. By doing this people often says nice things the other person didn't do on purpose and it begins to make relationships more positive.

Many parents get bogged down with thinking about the problems; they just need to take some action to remind themselves there are positives.

Positive can be found in unlikely places. For example a teenager being abusive and insulting to his mother may be praised for being comfortable enough to express his feelings and opinions.

Sometimes parents struggle to maintain a high quality of relationship with their child due to feeling that their child's behaviour is 'always bad' and there is 'nothing good'. To ensure a positive relationship it is important to find good in your child and keep a balanced perspective.

To help to ensure a positive image of your child there are a few things that can help. Taking time each day to remind yourself of what you love about your child; taking time to think about what your child enjoys and what they are good at; taking time to think about what their strengths are – like being strong willed, polite when they want to be, free thinking, etc.

Parents have a huge influence on their child's self-identity and self-esteem by the way they communicate. It is only through constantly praising effort (more importantly than praising the end result) and putting a positive and honest self-image on your child that helps your child take on that self-image.

Self-esteem is how good someone feels about themselves. Many parents want to get help to raise their child's self-esteem or to get their child anger management or counselling to find out 'why' they lack self-esteem or 'why' they are always so angry or 'why' they behave bad.

The best way to lift self-esteem, reduce anger and bad behaviour is to constantly and consistently honestly praise your child.

The reason for praising effort more than the end result is that research has shown when people only get praised for success it builds an 'all or nothing' mind set which in children can lead them to not try if they think they will fail which in some children can lead them to misbehave to avoid failure at a task.

The important thing is that they have done THEIR best; not that they have done THE best. You want the child to know that as long as they have done the best they could do and tried their hardest that you are proud. This goes for all areas of their life and behaviour.

Parents can sometimes focus on the negatives neglecting the positives. So for example if your child keeps truanting from school and misses four out of five days of school per week you can focus on praising them for that one day they attend.

You will have consequences in place for the non-attendance that you will have made clear to the child and you will already have told them why it is important to attend school so there isn't much use focusing heavily on this. It is better to have the consequence in place and remind them of the consequence and then focus on the positives.

It could be for example that the child earns £1 per day for each day they attend school and they get what they earn at the weekend. The consequences of not attending 4 out of 5 days are that they only get £1 at the weekend. But you can praise them for the day they attended and if one week they attend two days you can praise them for this. So you are constantly building a positive relationship between yourself and your child built on honest praise, love, holding a positive image of your child in mind and working at maintaining a view of your child through those 'positive glasses' whilst at the same time demonstrating that there are boundaries and there are consequences to not sticking to the boundaries but all of what the parent does is based on love and keeping a safe and secure nurturing environment for the child.

Listening and Communication

To improve communication and listening use 'I' statements rather than 'you' so explain how you feel about the behaviour rather than saying 'you...'

Make what you say specific. So if they have done something wrong only talk about that one thing. Don't bring in past experiences. Avoid terms like 'you always...' 'you never...' etc... as these terms imply that things are always this way and are unchanging and more importantly they imply that this is 'who you are' rather than this being about a current behaviour in a current situation that may or may not happen again and hasn't always happened in the past; that if you think hard enough you could probably find at least one exception where they did tidy their bedroom, help with the washing up, etc.

Find ways to offer you child areas of freedom and control over the decisions made. Offer choices and be willing to negotiate. When your child is being good make a conscious effort to spend time with them. If they appear upset or like they could do with someone to talk to offer to talk even if they tell you they don't want to. If they say they don't want to say something like 'OK, if you change your mind I will just be downstairs, come and find me' very often they will talk at this point. If your child wants to talk and you are busy don't turn them away explain you are busy and that you will be free in 'x' minutes or if they want to talk now they can help you with what you are doing while you both talk.

When you are talking with your child as far as possible focus on them as if they are the most important person in the World at that moment in time. Children normally open up and talk best when you are doing something with them. It could be that you are in a car together, or making something together or watching TV. They often feel more relaxed when they don't have to make eye contact. Remember not to judge them or over react or try to offer advice unless they have asked for it but to listen and feedback helpfully.

For example if a child said they were in a shop and their friend stole something and they didn't know what to do. Some parents may 'flare up' and try to tell the child not to spend time with that friend. The more useful response would be something like 'it sounds like that was a really difficult situation to be in'. This praises the child and allows them to feel un-judged and to carryon talking.

Remember to find ways to give your child freedom, to negotiate, to give them a sense of control, and to offer them choices

Help with getting your child to sleep

Over the years I have developed a number of highly effective strategies for helping children to sleep. Firstly you can put the house to sleep. By this I mean a few hours before the child's bedtime you begin to draw curtains, turn down lights, quieten the home, and turn music and TV down. Begin to talk 'implying' bedtime by asking things like 'do they want a drink before bed? Do they want a snack (toast etc) before bed? Do they want a bath before bed or a shower in the morning?' Also you can turn the heating down a little this will increase the chances of them wanting to go to bed.

Another idea I have used hundreds of times successfully with younger children (up to about 10 years old and some teenagers but less frequently) is to put on relaxation or guided meditation CD's. Even if the child doesn't understand the track they pick up on the non-verbal messages (relaxing tone of voice etc) and begin to drift off (this is very good if your child worries a lot as it focuses the mind on something other than the worrying). Read to your child at night and as you read imagine you are getting tired and sleepy, yawn a few times, as you read slow down, relax and deepen your tone of voice so that as you read your child will begin to relax to your voice rather than reading with an exciting or adventurous voice.

Or the most effective technique is to offer to sit quietly with your child until they fall asleep. And as you do gently stroke their arm (up in time with each in breath and down in time with each out breath) at the same time breathe in time with their breathing. Then after doing this a while begin to 'lead' your child to sleep by making the strokes slightly longer and breathing slightly deeper. Again it helps to imagine you are getting tired and sleepy. Don't leave the room until your child is showing signs they have fallen asleep (eye movement under their eyelids, a change in breathing pattern, twitches in the hands, legs etc).

With teenagers it is harder to make them fall asleep. Generally teenagers should be learning to make their own decisions and should be taking responsibility for their own actions. If strategies like 'putting the house to sleep' don't seem to work. Or the problem is that the teenager is often out late then as a parent the most likely answer is to think about natural consequences like the teenager being late for school or college, or being tired when woken up in the morning and not given a chance to lay in bed all day so that over time they are becoming increasingly tired and eventually just need to fall asleep at bedtime.

The other option that frequently works well is to tell the child to stay awake. Everybody has had the experience of trying to stay awake for a TV programme they want to watch only to find they fall asleep, or to try to fall asleep only to discover they can't sleep. This psychological principle can be helpful to use with children and young people.

With younger children you can sit in their bedroom and be watching TV together (something calming, never something with 'action' or lots of humour or anything else which raises energy levels) and you can suggest to the child something like 'I really want to know what happens in this programme but I'm so tired I might fall asleep. If I do begin to fall asleep can you make sure you stay awake to watch to the end of the programme so that you can tell me what happens.' Then as you watch the programme begin to 'feel sleepy and relaxed', yawn, struggle to keep your eyes open etc.

With older children or teenagers you can suggest they stay up a bit later or not to go to bed until ....x... (Whatever time they would normally go to bed themselves). I have on occasion even suggested they try to stay up all night. Even if they manage it as long as you don't let them sleep during the day the next day they will be tired the following night and more likely to go to bed at an appropriate time.

Reducing the risk of aggression

There are a number of useful techniques and skills that you can learn to reduce the risk of aggression and to de-escalate situations.

Thinking before you speak, not winding your child up

So often people say what they think without thinking about how that communication is going to be received. It could be an unhelpful comment or it could be a comment that appears argumentative.

By thinking before speaking the communication you give is likely to be more productive. There are a number of other advantages to thinking before speaking. When you do this you slow down your responses, this makes you look calmer. You also are more likely to be listening to what the child has to say because you will give more periods of silence.

People are often uncomfortable with silence yet when you are it gives more time for the other person to think and calm down.

When communicating it is better to use 'What', 'When', 'Where', 'How' questions rather than 'Why' questions. Many parents ask their child 'why did you do that?' When you ask a 'why' question it can sound accusing. 'Why' questions also are asking for an opinion rather than a factual piece of information and often the child doesn't know why.

For example; imagine a child sat in the living room watching television, and then they suddenly become aggressive. You ask why and they respond with 'I don't know' and you are left thinking 'he is always getting aggressive for no reason, there sometimes isn't even a trigger and he doesn't even know why'.

If you ask him 'what were you doing before you just kicked off?' and continue with 'what' questions he can tell you he was sitting watching something on TV and then felt he was getting anxious and then just lashed out. As the parent you can then have a greater chance of working out how what he was doing led to his behaviour.

Keeping your child informed or involved

When you keep people involved and informed it makes people feel respected and valued. It also takes away a key piece of potential fuel for any aggression. They are less likely to argue that you didn't tell them what was going on. They may still be annoyed about a situation but are more likely; especially teenagers; to understand.

For example;

If a child is waiting for an appointment and there is a delay, if the child knows they are likely to remain calm for longer. Or if you have to do some shopping or pick up a prescription etc and haven't told the child they are more likely to be anxious than if you explained what you were doing and had them involved in decision making.

People like to feel that they are being involved and consulted, not ignored.

Offering good choices

In many situations parents make the mistake of only offering negative options.

To offer good choices you need to make sure that there are options that offer a way out for the child. If all of the options lead to negative outcomes then you are more likely to encounter problems or aggression.

In childcare I have known of many staff that would tell the children, if they didn't go to bed they would have their television removed from their room for a week. When the child didn't go to their room and they had their television removed they would play up every night for the whole week because they have nothing to lose.

When on the other hand the staff removed the television but said they could have it back when they have gone to bed on time three nights in a row, then the child would improve their behaviour because that is what gets them their television back. The control is in their hands not the hands of the staff. If they mess around night after night then they are choosing not to have their television back, it's not the staff making that decision.

An Understanding of Anger and how it controls the mind of the aggressor

Anger is a primal emotion that is designed to defend you from perceived threats. It is an emotion run by the most primitive part of your brain, the amygdala.

As it is such a primitive response it bypasses conscious thought and puts your body into fight mode about quarter of a second before the conscious rational part of you has a say in what is going on.

Everyone has had the experience of this happening, like when you hear something just behind you so you spin around in surprise ready to defend yourself against whatever is there only to notice that it was a branch moving in the wind, casting a shadow, rather than a threat. In the time it took you to turn around you had consciously received enough information to make the decision that there was really no threat, so you calm down.

If when your mind assesses the information it still perceives a threat then it won't stop the aggressive response. That aggressive response will grow into a narrow, fixed focus of attention on what it is that you feel you need to defend against.

In the past that normally would have been physical dangers like Lions or other tribes invading your land. Nowadays it is more likely to be anger in defence of ideas or beliefs. As these are threats that won't go away unless your opinion changes the anger that starts has no new immediate information to stop it.

I say immediate because it is the information just after the aggression begins that causes the decision to carry on or to calm down. Any information after this is too late. The anger will have taken control until the threat is gone or has burnt itself out.

When the anger takes control the aggressor enters a highly focused state of mind. The more intelligent parts of their mind don't get accessed. This causes black or white thinking. It causes a state or mind where there is no grey. 'You are right they are wrong'. It reduces your intelligence because your thinking doesn't have access to the more advanced communication centres of your brain.

It is for these reasons that you can't reason with the angry person because they will not see other points of view.

It is important to realise that the fight or flight response which is happening in the aggressive person is also happening in the person that is facing the aggression.

How you feel physically inside is also how the aggressive person is feeling inside. The difference is how you are using these feelings and this response. Physically it is the same response whether you get scared and run or get angry and fight. Another option that can happen is that you can freeze. This is also a survival response. Many animals drop to the ground when they are attacked and 'play dead'. When for example the Lion that just chased down the gazelle has caught the gazelle, which collapses to the ground, the lion can then go and get her young before returning. In this brief window of opportunity the gazelle can get up, shake out the built up energy and run back to join its herd.

The physiological effects that you will both be experiencing are:

- When you experience fear or anger your body floods with stress hormones like adrenaline and noradrenalin
- You get a release of sugar and fat by the liver to increase the amount of energy in your body ready for fighting or running
- Breathing speeds up to give you more oxygen
- Blood rushes to the muscles in the arms and legs and to the brain to prepare you to run or stand and fight
- The heart speeds up and blood pressure rises to help ensure that oxygenated blood gets to where it is required
- Your muscles tense up as they prepare to be used

- Non essential bodily functions shut down, functions that are not necessary for immediate survival like digestion and saliva production. This can cause feelings of a dry mouth, butterflies in your stomach and loosening of the bowels and bladder
- Your senses become heightened and time can often seem to slow right down which allows you to make quick decisions or take rapid action
- Your pupils dilate which lets more light in allowing you to take in more information

Often after incidents have occurred these effects are still lingering and can make you feel uncomfortable and perhaps feeling like maybe you are having a panic attack. You are not. It is just the residual effects of these changes. If you shake yourself or do something active this can help to reduce the effects and calm you down. After an incident your body doesn't just instantly return to normal. It can take five to ten minutes to begin to feel calmer. The effects will last longer than this out of your awareness but your breathing and pulse will normally be more relaxed in that space of time.

If your child has either got really frustrated or angry they can also do something active to get the energy out of their body and begin to calm down. Because the residual effects last for a number of hours it is easy to reignite the aggression or anxiety so it is best to do all you can to keep things calm for a number of hours and not discuss any issues until many hours later or even the next day.

It is a myth that letting out aggression calms you down. If someone is encouraged to be aggressive to try to let the aggression out it makes them more likely to continue to be aggressive. It may in the short term make them calm because of exhaustion but it is also reinforcing the pattern of aggression. This is especially the case if someone is told to think of what is making them angry and to let it out at a punch bag or pillow etc. If it was true that thinking of something whilst being aggressive stopped the aggression towards that thing (for example a child feeling anger towards a parent) then boxers would get in the ring and hug because they would have 'let all of their aggression out' when punching the punch bag while thinking about the other boxer they hope to defeat.

The antidote to aggression is relaxation. By learning to relax you free up the higher part of the brain to 'work through' and resolve problems and also begin to train the brain to respond that way in the future instinctively.

Basic emotional needs

If you have an awareness of the basic emotional needs that people have you can begin to know what situations are likely to be most conducive to causing an increase of violence or aggression and what situations are likely to reduce violence or aggression, or even lead to a calmer environment.

By being aware of the needs of your child you may find it quicker and easier to know what needs to change or happen to resolve situations. Likewise if you are aware of the basic emotional needs you can notice what needs to change to make the environment or situation better for yourself.

When your needs are met you will have a higher tolerance to stress

The same applies for your child; if their personal needs are all met appropriately then they are less likely to get aggressive and if they do become aggressive they are more likely to calm down quicker and be easier to deal with.

Some of the main basic emotional needs are:

1. The need to give and receive attention

We all have a need to get a certain level of attention. If someone feels that they are not getting enough attention then there is an increased chance of that person being involved negatively in situations. It could be that they feel ignored so has a lower tolerance to other family members, friends or teachers and snap at them more. Or they could be receiving a lack of attention at home or be in a situation where no-one is acknowledging them so they feel they are being ignored, which could lead to an incident. Any lack of attention can lead to a craving for the attention or despondency due to not having the attention, some people will begin to change character and play up and may even become aggressive, while others will change and get withdrawn.

2. The mind body connection

If anyone gets reduced sleep or reduced exercise they are likely to become more mentally lethargic and more prone to stress and anger. They are likely to snap more due to having less tolerance.

If on the other hand anyone is happy for some reason or kept jolly or laughing then they are likely to be more stress free and more tolerant to others around them. They will appear far more capable of coping.

Also the more stressed people get the less tolerance they have to physical pain and at the same time the more chance they have of suffering aches and pains and headaches. Whereas a relaxed person will be more tolerant to pain, they will also be less likely to experience pain.

3. The need for purpose and goals

Everybody has a need for purpose and goals. Not just for the rewards specifically but because we are all hardwired to need a purpose and to want things to achieve. When someone becomes aggressive they will have a purpose or an agenda set out that they plan on following. Depending on their age and understanding they may not have this formulated into words just ideas of what they want that has led them to behave the way they are.

To keep stress down it is useful to have small achievable goals. This applies to parenting and not trying to do everything at once and keeping things in small manageable chunks; and it applies to helping your child by helping them to learn to break things down to smaller chunks. This can sometimes be useful by having the child frequently feel they have achieved something that is a step in the direction of something they want. Each time they achieve something they know they are more likely to get what they want and each frequent achievement is something they want.

4. Connection to something bigger than yourself

It is a human trait that we want a connection to something bigger than ourselves (whether a religion or a group or a cause). Your child will want to fit in; they are likely to want to join a gang or have a close circle of friends, and to want to fit in with the family (the amount of fitting in with family varies with age. A younger child will want to please family, whereas teenagers will normally only want family around when they are upset and want emotional support or to do things for them). This will serve many purposes' including to meet many of these needs. If anyone becomes outcast they are likely to become emotional and feel they don't belong. This can lead to a depressed mood, resentment and anger.

5. The need for stimulation and creativity

Again as us humans are hardwired with a need for stimulation and creativity, if this is denied it is likely to lead to boredom, anxiety and stress. In situations where not a lot happens and boredom can set in easily people may create games to play to meet this need or begin to play up to try to get some stimulation of any kind.

6. The need to feel understood and connected

If people get along this need gets met. If the family communicate well and do things together this need is likely to get met. If on the other hand anyone is excluded from the family and doesn't get on with anyone they are likely to quickly get quite down and appear to be quite low.

If this need isn't met, for example; if someone tries to explain how they feel and tries to talk to their parents but doesn't get the help they are expecting then they may begin feeling that they have been rejected, and that no-one understands them.

There are many situations in which children feel they are not being listened to or understood. This can make them even angrier. The best course of action to take is to do your best to appear as helpful as possible. Agree with them as much as possible and if you have to disagree avoid saying things like 'yes, but…' as this makes people defensive.

7. The need to feel a sense of control

A sense of control is vital to all of us. In many situations unfortunately most of the control is taken away.

Children will try to give themselves control in their own ways. They may develop rituals or superstitions (like saying something before eating at meals, or arranging things in a specific way, or 'not stepping on cracks' or having a lucky item). Children that cope best with stress and situations are likely to create control in their mind. Parents should give every opportunity for the child to feel a sense of control while they set this freedom within the boundaries they specify.

The best way to manage situations and avoid aggression is to at least give the illusion of control to the people. For example giving a few options for the child to choose from, or as care staff we would offer a few choices of snacks to the children before they go to bed, or ask if they want to be woken at 0715 or 0730 in the morning and if they want a drink brought to their room when they wake up, or suggest as they've been good they can choose whether to go to bed at 1930 or 2000.

There are many ways to offer choices or find something a person has control over in a situation. If someone feels they have no control they may get aggressive, so help them to have control. When I used to work in childcare as a sanction for not getting up in time in the morning I would sometimes tell the child that if they didn't get up in fifteen minutes they would have their television removed from their room until they can show that they can get up on time three days in a row (I would have asked them to get up a number of times by this stage).

This sanction puts control on the child. If they get up they don't lose their television, if they don't get up they lose their television but can get it back in as little as three days. Or they could lose their television for longer if they continue to not get up. The choice is theirs, they are in control. The staff also win because the child has to learn to get up on time to get their television back and they also show that boundaries will be put in place and carried out.

What is necessary to remember when confronted with challenging behaviour

Control over yourself

It is important that you have control over yourself. When you are in a situation it is all too easy to begin to feel out of control. What you need to do is to learn how to step back in your mind and relax. Begin to take control of your breathing and how you are acting.

Learn to do 7-11 breathing. This is where you breathe in to the count of 7 and out to the count of 11. What this does is it sets off the relaxation response. It can also be useful to consciously let your shoulders relax.

Control how you respond before any incident even begins. So many parents say things that can be overheard causing the situation to escalate or due to their expectations the situation goes how it is expected to go.

For example:

Saying 'here she comes, better prepare yourself for trouble'

Or

'He never settles on time, it always leads to problems'

Clearly if you have an attitude that things will go wrong or if you say things that can be overheard there is an increased chance of those things happening.

Don't take anything personally

When someone is being aggressive towards you they don't really know what they are saying. They have an agenda. They are fighting for what at that time they believe to be right.

Part of this fighting maybe to attack you verbally

If you start to take what is said to you personally then you are likely to begin to get annoyed and angry also. What you need to do is understand that it doesn't matter what is said to you.

I have heard so many times people being put down, insulted, threatened, and emotionally attacked. It is important to remain calm and just focus on the situation at hand. Remember anything hurtful or upsetting that is being said is just to get a reaction and by responding to it you will be fuelling the fire.

Forward Planning

Hindsight is a wonderfully useful thing so why not start with it. If you plan in advance how you will respond in situations or what various outcomes are possible and what might cause problems to occur you can reduce risks and plan better ways of managing situations.

You can also frequently practice how you will handle situations in your mind so that if they happen you have had lots of practice and have a good idea of how things will go and what you will do.

People are only human and will occasionally make mistakes. This is normal. The important thing is to reflect on situations and on how they could be handled differently next time and what would have to have happened for the situation to have gone well or better.

Strategies for managing challenging behaviour

The idea of these strategies is to avoid the situation leading to aggression.

Offering support, when someone is beginning to get frustrated

Often when your child is beginning to get frustrated it can help to offer support. Offering support can make them feel calmer as they can feel that you are working with them not against them.

When you offer support it is best to try to both sit down to talk. This will help to calm the situation down, as sitting is a calming action whereas standing is more active. You can start by feeding back what your child says to show that you understand them. If what you feed back is wrong then they have the opportunity to correct you.

Distraction

Distraction is a useful way of stopping the build up of aggression. Everyone has had the experience of having something on their mind that they are about to say and just as they go to say it someone cuts in and says something else or they say something like 'hang on a minute I've just got to do this'. And when they ask you what you wanted to say you find that you have forgotten.

To use distraction effectively it works best to be a non-threatening distraction and one that your child would be happy to accept. It also works best if you do it by timing an interruption well.

Reassurance that you will do what you can

Offering reassurance to someone that is becoming aggressive is a useful technique for seeming to come alongside your child and show that you will do your best to help them sort out their situation.

Remember though that you don't want to take away any of their developmental opportunities. You only want to do what you can based on what your child says they would like you to help them with.

Many parents get told something by their child and respond by trying to solve the problem even though the child hasn't asked for that. You want to give them the chance to do what they can and only help in the areas they want help with. Obviously this will vary depending on the child's understanding of a situation.

For example if a child comes home from school saying they were bullied many parents respond by trying to sort it out, contacting other parents, teachers etc. Yet the child hasn't asked for this. So although the parents are doing all this because they love their children they are taking away opportunities for the child to learn for themselves.

It may be that the child was bullied but that by the end of the day they get on fine with the other child and that by rushing in there to sort out the situation it has a negative impact. It is more important to just ask 'is there anything I can do to help?' or 'how would you like me to help?'

Often even if you fail to resolve the situation or are unable to help the fact that they have seen that you tried your best will lead to your child being grateful for your help.

Planned ignoring like walking away with a reason

When someone is angry they are very focused and one-minded. This means that they don't always listen or see alternative points of view. If you take yourself out of a situation leaving your child alone in the situation they have no one to be angry with and so they often will begin to calm down.

When they are calm enough they will be more likely to listen to what you have to say.

Planned ignoring is a key strategy to use whether it is saying 'I'm just going to the other room to give you time to calm down. I'll come back in five minutes to see how calm you are' or whether you say something like 'I've just got to make a quick call then I'll be straight back. It should only take about five minutes' or 'When you have calmed down so that we can talk about this then I will talk with you'

With children and young people it is important that you make them aware that you will talk to them when they talk to you calmly and not when they are shouting, swearing and demanding from you. There are times when you may let swearing slide a little for example when they have received bad news and are angry and not in control of what they are saying.

If you try to stop them swearing then it won't work. You need to show you are listening and use other strategies and when they have calmed enough to respond to you then you can mention not swearing.

Planned ignoring based on the behaviour when the child or young person is in a high state of anger is less likely to work than giving an excuse to temporarily remove yourself from the situation.

It is important to make sure that the child still feels you care. Planned ignoring isn't the same as just ignoring. You are conveying the message that you want to talk with the child and help them and that you care about them, while at the same time letting them know that some behaviour is acceptable and other behaviour isn't.

Removing an audience

Removing an audience helps to calm down situations with young people and children. With children and young people if there is an audience they are more likely to play up to it so by removing the audience they are likely to calm down more.

Removing the audience can be done by having everyone moving from the situation. It could be by saying something like 'why don't we go to the lounge and get ready to watch the film'.

Or you can move your child to a different room. To do this you could just simply suggest something like, 'why don't we move to the other room. It's a little quieter in there so we can talk properly', or 'why don't we go just round the corner to get out of the noise'.

Offering some time to calm down

Sometimes it can be useful to offer some time to someone to allow them to calm down before talking with them. When people calm down they begin to see more rationally.

If you are going to offer time for someone to calm down remember to say how long you will be away while they are calming or where they can find you when they are calmer.

This is a technique that works well for children. Giving them time to calm down before you will talk with them.

It could be that you suggest they sit in a room perhaps like the dining room to calm down.

It is important with children or young people not to send them to their own room if possible because they will build the association between being anxious or aggressive and being in their room.

You want them to associate calming and sleeping with their own bedroom.

Choices

Whenever you create choices in your child's mind you start breaking down any anger. This is because when they are angry they are in a focused state of mind and only see black and white. By creating choices in their mind you start creating greys this brings the rational part of the mind back into play which starts to dissolve the anger.

Choices often aren't readily taken on board when offered to someone that is highly aggressive but it does work well to start to prevent anger from continually escalating.

You want to make sure that there are positive choices that can be taken and preferably options that allow your child to not lose face or feel they had to back down.

Negotiating

Another strategy is negotiating with your child before they become too aggressive. Being prepared to perhaps compromise like rather than demand that your child cleans their room and have them continue to argue and get more aggressive about not wanting to, you could offer to help them.

Setting boundaries

By having boundaries in place that are all agreed and stuck to by the whole family the children know what they can and can't do. If there have been no boundaries in place then to start with the children may become more challenging as they try to fight against the new boundaries to find out if they will be maintained.

After a short period of time the children will be used to the boundaries and will accept them. Without boundaries children may be difficult at bedtimes and not settle they may ignore everything that they are told. It is important that any response to broken boundaries doesn't remove choices.

Changing the parent

Sometimes your child being aggressive may be aiming all of their anger at one parent. In these situations it can be useful to find a way of changing to the other parent dealing with the behaviour. This also works to cause a little distraction. It can also work using other adults like a Grandparent or a close friend or relative.

Maintaining or setting routines

Routines are important for aiding stability. When people don't have a set routine they can begin to feel uncomfortable because they feel a lack of security and structure. With children especially they are much calmer when they receive meals at regular times and get woken and go to bed at regular times.

If they have ADHD or Asperger's or OCD they are more likely to behave better when there is a clear set routine.

By creating regular routines you will minimise anger build up. Without a clear routine there can be an increased feeling of uncertainty which can lead to increased anger and frustration.

Finally

All of the ideas in this book have been used personally in thousands of situations when dealing with challenging behaviour. They have been used by many colleagues of mine over the years and have been taught to thousands of parents that have successfully put these ideas and strategies into practice.

The most important thing to remember is to be reflective on your situation. You want to make time for yourself to look at what you do as a parent and what the problems are, what strategies you use that don't work and most importantly what you use that does work and how situations have ended.

Look for what you do differently when things get resolved.

You want to make sure that the parenting message is the same from all parents (or adults like Grandparents etc…) involved so that the child is getting a clear and consistent message.

You want to develop an authoritative parenting style. This is a parenting style where you put boundaries firmly in place with consequences and you also think about your child and their needs. So consequences will be appropriate, negotiation will take place with your child, they will have choices, etc.

Below is a selection of questions you should regularly ask yourself. It is useful to write the questions down when you get stuck and to then write down the answers. Often parents find these questions can help to lead to some clarity:

What would you like?

What is different about the times when…? (What you'd like is happening)

What do you do to help make that happen?

How does it make your day go differently? (When that happens)

Who else notices that…and what do they notice? (When that happens things go well)

How did you get…to stop/end…? (Eg, Johnny to calm down)

How did you figure out that…(to stop this)…you needed to …(do this)

Have you ever had this difficulty in the past? (Similar problem with another child, etc…)

(Yes) How did you resolve it then? What do you need to do to get that to happen again? (What is stopping you from doing the same again?)

What will be the very first sign that things are moving in the right direction? (Or sign that things are continuing in the right direction?) Then what…? (What would happen next, and next. Getting a series of stages and building up a picture of success)

What are some of the positive things about your child? If you were told to convince someone what a good child they are what would you say?

Keep a record of positive things that happen with your child. It could be times they have done something nice for you, or times they have made you proud, or times someone else has praised them (or praised you for their behaviour).

When people are having difficulties it can be a challenge to think there is any good. So this last part is something parents can do so that they can see things aren't always bad. You need to do it honestly and take time to find positives if in your mind the first response was that there aren't any.

1610575R0

Printed in Great Britain
by Amazon.co.uk, Ltd.,
Marston Gate.